FACES OF RAILROADING

FACES OF RAILROADING

Portraits of America's greatest industry | Carl A. Swanson

KALMBACH
BOOKS

Printed in Canada

04 05 06 07 08 09 10 11 12 13   10 9 8 7 6 5 4 3 2 1

Publisher's Cataloging-in-Publication
(Provided by Quality Books, Inc.)

Swanson, Carl, 1960-
   Faces of railroading : portraits of America's
greatest industry / Carl Swanson. — 1st ed.
   p. cm.
   ISBN 0-87116-208-3

   1. Railroads—United States—Pictorial works.
I. Title.

TF149.S93 2004   385'.0973
                        QBI03-200945

Art Director: Kristi Ludwig

Cover photo: Ward Kimball
Page 2 photo: Martin Lutton

photo | Jim Shaughnessy

Acknowledgments

Many people had a hand in producing this book.
In particular I would like to thank Kevin Keefe,
Dick Christianson, and Kent Johnson for proposing
this project and helping shape its development,
Julia Gerlach and Candice St. Jacques for their
skillful editing, and art director Kristi Ludwig for
turning a manuscript and a stack of photographs
into a cohesive and visually appealing work.

Dedication

For Judy and our wonderful children John,
Daniel, and Rachel.

TABLE OF CONTENTS

Preface 9

Introduction 11

The Faces of Railroading
Essay by Doug Riddell
Amtrak locomotive engineer

chapter one 14

The Hogger, The Tallowpot, and The Captain
No matter what you call 'em, engineers, firemen, and conductors kept the wheels of commerce turning

chapter two 38

Time Machine
Before 1883, every city and town set its own time, but that was no way to run a railroad

chapter three 44

Down at the Station
From "tank-town" depots to metropolitan landmarks, a ticket to adventure awaited all who stepped across the platform

It's train time and men young and old head down the platform to better witness the departure of this Central Vermont Railway passenger train from White River Junction, Vermont, in September 1951.

photo | A.C. Kalmbach

chapter four 56

Riding the Great Trains
Whether traveling aboard lowly commuter trains or lordly streamliners, passengers enjoyed rail travel in its heyday

chapter five 82

The Guiding Hand
Dispatchers, tower operators, and railroad officials directed an empire from behind the scenes

The Rights of Trains
Essay by Mark W. Hemphill
Editor, *Trains* Magazine

chapter six 98

The Permanent Way
Back-breaking work by an army of men built and maintained the railroad

chapter seven 114

Yard Work
When it came to moving freight, yards and the men who worked them made it happen

Greeted by well-wishers, Southern Pacific engineer Bascom Farrow climbs down from his last run in 1948, capping a railroad career that began in 1900. The photographer, Ward Kimball, one of Walt Disney's original animators, also took the photograph of Bascom Farrow that appears on the cover.

photo | Ward Kimball

chapter eight 132

Roundhouse and Backshop
Some of America's most skilled craftsmen tended to the care and feeding of steam and diesel iron horses

Afterword 160

Preface

The railroad is an American icon. Railroads settled America and then unified the country in a web of steel. For many people, especially prior to the development of the automobile, the locomotive's whistle echoing across hills and fields symbolized unfettered freedom of movement as well as a smaller, less-isolated world.

To work the railroad, to tame those gigantic machines, took strength, intelligence, and guts. Railroad engineers, firemen, brakemen, and conductors became our national heroes. They were at the forefront of progress and their hard work was evident in their hands, their sweat-stained clothes, their faces.

America's greatest industry has been well-documented in photographs. Highly skilled photographers captured the trains, the stations, the workshops, and the scenery on film. Most importantly, they photographed the people who built and used the railroads, from the engineers and conductors to the porters and passengers.

The full story of working for America's railroad industry is beyond the scope of this book. A thoughtful exploration of attitudes toward, for example, race and gender, would be an immensely complex undertaking. A single railroad company may link diverse regions of the country and its corporate traditions may stretch back a century or more. Railroading is a geographic and historical pageant, played out on a continental stage, and filled with ever-shifting subplots. Even the sometimes cooperative, sometimes fractious relations between workers and management defy generalization. Only those who lived it can fully tell the story, and the story is different for every one of the untold thousands who toiled in sweat and smoke. The photographs in this book give us a glimpse into the working lives of these people and shed a ray of light on the labor and love that created the steel web connecting our communities.

Several of the images in this book were produced by company photographers and were usually painstakingly arranged and posed. In these images, we see the face of railroading as the railroad companies wished it to be perceived. Other photographs in this book were created by amateur photographers who found in this dynamic industry the spark that kindled their creativity. Almost all the images were created in the middle decades of the twentieth century, when improvements in cameras and film combined with a new understanding of photography as an art form to produce documentary photography of exceptional power. The artistry of these photographers, both amateur and professional alike, made this book possible.

In 1949, strong backs and a long wrench
made short work of the job of tightening bolts
on the crossing of the Nickel Plate and
Chesapeake & Ohio railroads at Fostoria, Ohio.

photo | Richard J. Cook

Introduction

The Faces of Railroading

by Doug Riddell

Amtrak locomotive engineer

I've given up trying to explain my career to non-railroaders. They don't understand why I leave home, family, friends, and social obligations on a moment's notice when the crew clerk summons me to another run. They don't understand why a call to duty is just as likely to come in the middle of the night as it is in the middle of the day, or in the middle of a first date, or in the middle of a friend's last rites.

A railroader's love for the job is even hard to explain to other railroaders. Between trips we'll sit in the lobby of a shabby hotel and talk about our pre-railroad lives. Sooner or later we'll pose the inevitable question: "Are we better off?" Certainly there is no end to the hardships and dangers of our profession. Even the elements conspire against us.

On September 26, 1985, I was called to run a freight train of urgently needed auto parts to a truck assembly plant in Norfolk, Virginia, which was directly in the path of Hurricane Gloria. With our mission accomplished, we learned that our managers had reneged on a promise to get our crew home before the storm hit. Instead, we were dropped off at a motel in Portsmouth, Virginia, to ride out the hurricane. When large objects and small animals started flying past the hotel's rattling plate glass windows, we called the chief train dispatcher and told him we had placed letters in the motel safe directing our families to sue the railroad in the event of our deaths. Moments later a limousine battered its way through the storm to whisk us up Interstate 64 to Richmond. I could see waves breaking over the deck of the Hampton Roads Bridge ahead of us as the dreadnought Caddie swayed and rocked in the buffeting winds, and I wondered if I had challenged fate once too often.

Fate answered a few days later. The emergency auto parts run had disrupted my work schedule, and the engineer substituting on my regular run hit a school bus at a road crossing. The bus driver was killed and the young bus passengers and substitute engineer were left physically and mentally scarred for life.

Recently, and despite a lifetime witnessing the cursing, the anger, and the broken promises that are part and parcel

Doug Riddell, locomotive engineer

photo | Doug Riddell

of the job, my son Ryan has joined the fraternity of the high iron. I burst with pride every time I see Ryan in his Amtrak assistant conductor's uniform, but I fear for his future, his safety, and his well-being. When our trains pass, I pick up the radio handset and remind Ryan, "Be careful, be safe, and get your rest." Because a railroader never knows when the phone is going to ring.

Yet it's the path my son has chosen to follow, just as I followed my grandfather, Chesapeake & Ohio Railway conductor John Everett Beazley, down aisles of the C&O's crack passenger train, the *George Washington*. When I was a kid, Richmond's Main Street Station and Fulton Yard was a second home to me. The engineers, conductors, and porters were my extended family, and I knew them all by name. When the army of car men, pipe fitters, and electricians descended to couple the *George Washington*'s locomotives to its cars, the din of their hammers attacking stubborn steam connections, brake hoses, and signal lines was music to my ears.

Railroading truly has a magical side, and as my son Ryan grew up, that's the side of railroading he knew. He wasn't yet born when I made my first run as a locomotive fireman and was severely injured by a violent diesel-engine crankcase explosion. Nor was Ryan there in 1960 when the slack suddenly ran out of the couplings between 200 empty coal hoppers, throwing my grandfather from his caboose, breaking his back, ending his career, and eventually claiming his life. Grandpa's first railroad retirement check arrived the day of his funeral. It had to be returned—uncashed. Grandpa Beazley understood the dangers. Nearly everyone did. Once, a group of coal miners at a country store in West Virginia gasped when they discovered he worked for the railroad. The miners felt that sort of work was just too dangerous.

Grandpa's dream was for his grandson to work outside of railroading, to get a college education (which I did), and to learn a profession (which I also did, working for a time in broadcasting and advertising). But along with Grandpa's gold Hamilton 992B Railway Special watch, I inherited a fascination with trains and a respect for the profession. And just like that pocket watch that accompanied me my first day on the railroad, the love of railroading has now been passed along to a third generation.

What is it that draws us to the rails? For starters, it's looking back at the consist of the northbound *Silver Meteor* as it fades into a blowing curtain of new fallen snow at sunrise, the train braking gently and gliding over the frozen James River into Richmond at the end of a thankfully uneventful overnight journey. It's the aroma of beef stew and freshly baked corn muffins shared with a track gang during a break for lunch in the shady refuge of long-leaf Carolina Pines. It's head brakeman Henry Crump singing Ray Charles classics in the cab of a fast freight at 3 a.m. It's engineer Rob Yancey blasting the notes of "Mary's Baby Jesus" on the locomotive's five-chime air horn as he rolls homeward on December 24th in anticipation of the rare pleasure of being home when his family opens gifts around the Christmas tree. Those are the things that draw us to the rails.

And when you become an "old head" and step down for the last time, you will be torn between the desire to be free of the heartaches and stress and the reluctance to leave the railroad, the one constant in a nomadic life. For too many railroaders, there's never been time for anything else. The children your wife raised in your absence are grown and gone.

Ryan and Doug Riddell

John Everett Beazley

Your house may be paid for, but it's empty. So, before long you're visiting the crew room at the passenger station or the crew clerk's office at the freight yard. You delight in reminding your former co-workers that you sleep in your own bed each night. But you're there. You're back. You miss it.

And then there are the old-timers' picnics, the gatherings on crisp fall Saturday afternoons when the faces you've watched grow old still smile. However, like your own, they carry deepening age lines and ever-thickening eyeglasses. Joint replacements, necessitated by years of getting on and off moving trains, are a hot topic of discussion. Strong hands that once guided the *Champion* or the *Silver Star* now tremble as they lift a fork laden with apple pie.

There's a sense of loss when a co-worker with whom you've spent so much of your life fails to appear for the sweetened ice tea, barbecue, and Brunswick stew, and you hear from the whispers that he's answered life's last call.

Thanks to the hard work of dedicated photographers to put a human face on this industry, you will meet the people that made railroading great. If it's true that a picture is worth a thousand words, this look at the faces of railroading is indeed priceless. Join me as we stroll aisles, board engines, kick ballast, throw switches, and witness the world of the railroader. All aboard, my friends.

chapter one

The Hogger, The Tallowpot, and The Captain

No matter what you call 'em, engineers, firemen, and conductors kept the wheels of commerce turning

When a locomotive whistle wailed in the distance, the farmer whose horizon was framed by the flanks of his plow horses or the shopkeeper walled in by his wares may have longed to cast aside their familiar and confining lives for the freedom and excitement of the rails. Those who chose to follow this dream soon learned that romance is for outsiders...

The reality of the railroad industry is found in the pages of the rule book issued to every employee. Consider this five-sentence introduction, found on the opening page of the 1959 "Consolidated Code of Operating Rules," issued to every new employee of the Chicago, Milwaukee, St. Paul & Pacific Railroad.

"Safety is of the first importance in the discharge of duties.

"Obedience to the rules is essential to safety.

"To enter or remain in the service is an assurance of willingness to obey the rules.

"The service demands the faithful, intelligent and courteous discharge of duty.

"To obtain promotion, ability must be shown for greater responsibility."

Page upon page of rules follow this chilly welcome. Some of the rules are straightforward (Rule G: "The use of intoxicants or narcotics is prohibited."). Many of the rules are complex (Rule 27: "A signal imperfectly displayed or the absence of a signal at a place where a signal is normally displayed, must be regarded as the most restrictive indication that can be displayed at that signal, except that when a light is not burning on a signal and the day indication is plainly seen, or if an indication is displayed on a color light for the route to be used, it will govern.").

With more than a century of service to the Jersey Central behind them, engineer John Wait (right) and conductor Joseph T. Ross hold down the premier run on the line, the fast and ultra-luxurious *Blue Comet*, between New York City and Atlantic City, New Jersey.

photo I Kalmbach collection

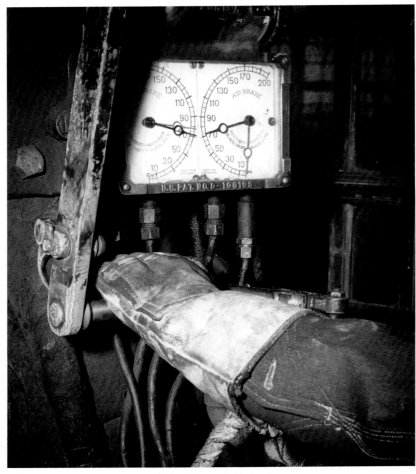

Engineers in the days of steam ran with a gloved hand on the throttle and a sharp eye on the air-brake gauges.

The rule book is deadly serious because railroading is a deadly serious business. One locomotive produces thousands of horsepower. A freight train can weigh more than 10,000 tons and take more than a mile to stop. A train has a thousand ways to kill or maim a careless worker. Skill, vigilance, and judgment born of years of experience are needed to control the beast.

It always was and still remains the ironclad belief of railroad managers that accidents caused by human error will be eliminated when every employee knows the rules thoroughly and applies them correctly in every instance. Neither the machines nor the management feel pity for a willfully careless worker.

After memorizing the rule book and passing an exhaustive test to prove they've done so, newly hired railroaders are finally able to "mark up" for their first run. They will remember this day for the rest of their lives because it establishes their seniority, and seniority determines the jobs they hold and if they will be laid off, possibly for years at a stretch, when business slows.

If times are good, they may find themselves working on a "chain gang" crew—running to a distant terminal, grabbing a few hours' rest, and then being called back to duty. The cycle repeats endlessly. It's a numbing, merciless schedule that leaves no time for friends, family, or hobbies. The railroad becomes their world.

Why do they do it? *Trains* magazine's long-time editor, the late David P. Morgan, studied that question and provided an eloquent answer in a 1953 essay. "The reward of the smoke and sweat is to hold in the palm of your gloved hand the throttle of a 189-ton Baldwin, to know that each notch of the curved ratchet overhead feeds more superheated steam into a pair of 28-inch-diameter cylinders with a 32-inch stroke, to realize that this rocking, pounding boiler stuffed with tubes and charged with more than 200-per-square-inch energy is yours to urge and restrain."

In this portrait of a veteran railroader, New York Central Railroad engineer Orrie D. Hopkins waits for the conductor's signal to depart. The passengers aboard this *Empire State Express* are in experienced hands. Mr. Hopkins joined the railroad in 1889, was promoted to engineer in 1902, and in 1936, after 47 years of service, finally accumulated enough seniority to hold down an elite passenger run. He retired in 1940.

photo | William P. Price

Before radios, train crews were dispatched by written instruction, delivered by hand from stations or towers spaced at intervals along their route. This is MY Tower at the Western Maryland Railway in March 1947. The tower operator has copied the dispatcher's telephoned orders, tied them with string to forked handles, and delivered one set to the engine crew. In this shot, he holds out an identical set to the conductor in the caboose as the train rolls past.

photo | Wayne Leeman

Before federal laws restricted hours of duty for train crews, cabooses were a crew's home away from home, but the conductor and brakeman rarely shared it with the engine crew of engineer and fireman, who laid over in boarding houses or railroad YMCAs. In the early years, train crews prepared and ate their meals in the caboose, a practice that has nearly disappeared today. Culinary talent varied from crew to crew, but the meals were hot and filling and depended heavily on fried bacon, eggs, potatoes, and coffee.

By the flickering yellow light of kerosene lanterns, a Frisco Lines conductor makes out his "wheel report," an accounting of the cars transported by his train, as his westbound fast freight train rumbles through Missouri on an April night in 1954.

photo | Wayne Leeman

On routes with too few riders to justify a passenger train, cabooses handled local package freight business and the occasional rider. This photo, taken in the 1950s, shows conductor H. M. (Bill) Sanders unloading freight at Mountain View, Missouri, on the Frisco Lines' 62-mile Current River Branch.

photo | Wayne Leeman

An engineer oils the bearings on his locomotive's 79-inch-diameter driving wheels before departing with an Indianapolis-Cleveland mail train in September 1955. Driver size determined speed: the larger the wheels, the faster the train. A 79-inch driver was almost as big as they came, and enabled speeds in excess of 100 mph.

photo | J. Parker Lamb Jr.

A Baltimore & Ohio Railroad fireman fills the tender of his locomotive at Flemington, West Virginia, in July 1956. Steam locomotives had a tremendous thirst and required frequent stops at lineside water tanks. When working hard, a steam locomotive could consume 3,000 or more gallons of water in two or three hours.

photo | James P. Gallagher

Engineers are responsible for basic repairs to their locomotives, and Bob Armstrong is taking advantage of a brief stop to venture out on the boiler catwalk and do a little fine-tuning.

photo | Frank Clodfelter

Shovel by shovel, ton after ton, this Pennsylvania Railroad fireman does his part to convert the coal in the tender to horsepower.

photo | Don Wood

Engineer George Miley worked regular assignments for a Louisiana short line into his late 70s. This photograph was taken in 1950. The spartan and functional accommodations of his steam-locomotive cab are typical.

photo | C.W. Witbeck

photo | Wallace W. Abbey

The engineer and conductor of Erie Railroad train number 6 compare their watches shortly before the train leaves Dearborn Station in Chicago bound for New York City.

A Pennsylvania Railroad locomotive makes a late-night servicing stop at Elmira, New York, in 1956. In addition to coal and water, the locomotive takes on sand, which is sprayed under the engine's driving wheels when additional traction is needed,

photo | Jim Shaughnessy

Vinton, Virginia, east of Roanoke, lies at the west end of the Norfolk & Western Railway's Blue Ridge grade, a geographic obstacle to the flood of coal running from coal mines in West Virginia to ocean docks in Norfolk, Virginia. Here, pusher locomotives coupled on to boost trains up the hill. Late at night in summer 1958, a pusher crew chats in the hot, humid air, awaiting the arrival of the train they'll help.

photo | Jim Shaughnessy

photo | Dan Sanborn

In this 1952 photo, a Louisville & Nashville fast freight bound for Atlanta, Georgia, from Corbin, Kentucky, rockets past a Cincinnati-bound freight that has taken the side track to let the faster train pass.

The arrival of diesel locomotives like this 1,500-horsepower engine built for the Gulf, Mobile & Ohio Railroad, freed engineers from the grime and heat of steam locomotives, but the engineer's job still demands vigilance, experience, and good judgment.

photo | Jacob Lofman

photo | Frank Clodfelter

Southern Railway engineer Joe Sawyer pours a drink of coffee during a rare quiet moment in the cab. A glass bottle of coffee (snug against the hot boiler) and a tin cup were standard equipment on Joe's engine.

The photographer, a one-time locomotive fireman, wrote on the back of this photo, "Joe finished his life with the most carefree face I have ever noted. He faced every situation with quiet dignity and treated everyone with respect. I hope this photo reveals the look of a quiet man we called 'Southern Gentleman.'"

Room with a view? Not in the cab of a steam locomotive. At the best of times, the long boiler and shoebox-sized windshield hampered visibility. Add a layer of soot and flying grease and sometimes it's just easier to lean out when you need a clear look at the tracks ahead.

photo | Robert Hale

photo | George W. Gerhart

Reading Company steam locomotives were being put out to pasture by new diesel locomotives in the early 1950s. This fireman on the locomotive tender isn't going to let it happen without a fight, though. Holding a hose, he carefully positioned himself to drench the passing diesel crew with water. Reports the delighted photographer, "He did, too!"

With layoffs and buyouts, mergers and line closures, and nights spent far from home, railroading is an unsettling line of work. On the other hand, there are moments like this peaceful winter day in California when railroading doesn't seem so bad.

photo | Jeff Brouws

chapter two

Time Machine

Before 1883, every city and town set its own time, but that was no way to run a railroad

Long before radios and extensive signaling systems, railroads safely and efficiently operated multiple trains on the same line. Supplied with timetables showing the schedules of all regular trains and precise written orders from the dispatcher, crews ran with a complete understanding of where and when they would meet other trains and which train would need to be in the siding to let the other pass.

The system worked because every employee had a reliable pocket watch and regularly compared it to a master clock that was known to be accurate. As a further safety check, crew members gathered before each run to "compare dials" and make sure each railroader's watch was correct.

By the mid-1800s, railroads were operating far-flung systems with split-second timing while the rest of the country considered the measurement of time's passage to be a purely local affair. Each community set its own time, often based on when the sun crossed the meridian when viewed from a local landmark. Solar time has a serious drawback, though: It varies depending on where you stand on the earth's surface. There is more than a minute's difference between solar noon at the eastern and western edges of Chicago. Another approach to setting time was to adopt the standard used by the local railroad. For example, the Pennsylvania Railroad scheduled its trains on Philadelphia time.

A passenger on a Pennsylvania Railroad train arriving in Baltimore discovered that the local time was five minutes behind Philadelphia. If that traveler planned to continue west on the Baltimore & Ohio Railroad, he would be wise to adjust his watch. The B&O ran its trains on Baltimore time—at least until it reached Ohio, where it switched to Columbus time, unless, of course, the train was west of Cincinnati, when it operated on Vincennes, Indiana, time.

Conductor H.C. Brown, engineer Van Santongue, and fireman Walter Thrall compare watches before leaving Los Angeles on Union Pacific streamliner *City of Los Angeles*. This is not just an empty ritual. These veteran railroaders know that lives may depend on precise timekeeping.

photo | Frank J. Peterson

The confusion multiplied in cities served by more than one railroad. Passengers in Buffalo, New York, were confronted by three station clocks. One was set to New York City time because that was the standard used by the New York Central Railroad. The second showed Columbus time for the convenience of Lake Shore & Michigan Southern passengers. And the third clock indicated local Buffalo time.

Residents of Buffalo had to keep the various times in mind when planning a journey, but they could take comfort in knowing the situation was even worse in Pittsburgh, which was served by railroads operating under six different time standards.

By the 1880s, the nation's railroads were using at least 68 different time standards, and even routine tasks, such as selling tickets for connecting trains, were becoming almost impossible.

Great Britain adopted Greenwich Mean Time in 1848. In the United States, several respected scientists had advocated dividing the nation into a handful of standard time zones, but little progress was made.

The railroads, far and away North America's dominant industry, decided it was time to flex their combined muscle. Acting with the overwhelming support of member railroads, William F. Allen, secretary of the American Railroad Association, announced four U.S. time zones: Eastern, Central, Mountain, and Pacific. Furthermore, the association stated, on Sunday, November 18, 1883, every railroad clock across the country would be set to the new time standard.

With the railroads unified, it didn't take long for the general public to accept standard time. In short order, local, state, and federal offices were also using the system promoted by the railroads, although it took Congress 35 more years to give official sanction to standard time.

Today, most trains are dispatched by radio, and their movements are controlled by color light signals. Nevertheless, every employee is still required to have a reliable watch, to compare it to a clock known to be accurate, and to make sure it never varies from the correct time by more than 30 seconds.

photo | Santa Fe Railway

Every railroad office where train crews reported to work was equipped with a standard clock by which railroaders set their watches. Each standard clock was checked daily by a special telegraph signal transmitted nationwide from the U.S. Naval Observatory in Washington, D.C. The card on the front of the clock case here indicates a one-second deviation from absolute accuracy. Note the two time zones.

photo | Santa Fe Railway

John Reich, a Santa Fe Railway clock maintainer at the railway's shops in Topeka, Kansas, notes that this clock is running fast. It will be corrected at once.

photo | Santa Fe Railway

photo | Richard Steinheimer

A section foreman of the Tidewater Southern Railway consults his Hamilton Railway Special at lunchtime for his gang near Escalon, California, in 1960. He will check the watch frequently because his gang has permission to work on the tracks for a fixed amount of time. When that time expires trains will start rolling, and his men had better be in the clear.

Here we see Chris Larsen of Santa Fe Railway's clock laboratory as he disassembles a time clock. The lower part of the mechanism is a recorder, a temperamental paper punch device that is very likely the source of this clock's woes.

chapter three

Down at the Station

From "tank-town" depots to metropolitan landmarks,
a ticket to adventure awaited all who stepped across the platform

Whether a modest small-town depot or the soaring stone halls of Grand Central Terminal, the train station from the mid-1800s to the mid-1900s was the centerpiece of many communities and a tangible symbol that travel and trade had replaced geographic isolation.

Small-town depots and big city terminals served very different functions, however. The combination freight and passenger station of small-town America typically faced a single track, each day handling a passenger or two, a sack of mail, and maybe a few milk cans. New York's Grand Central Terminal had 50 platform tracks, served 550 trains carrying one-half million passengers each day, and boasted that it was "the gateway to a continent."

The rural depot was presided over by an agent who sold the tickets, handled the luggage, manned the telegraph, stoked the potbelly stove to keep the waiting room warm in the winter months, and swept the floors and emptied the spittoons before locking up for the night. At Grand Central, 285 redcaps and 60 parcel attendants handled the baggage, a 335-person cleaning staff kept the cavernous halls tidy, and 45 terminal police officers kept the multitudes safe.

Which of the two stations is more important to its community? The hands-down winner is the little wooden building at the end of the branch line. If the residents of a remote hamlet had dealings with the world beyond the town limits, they talked to the station agent. If they needed two empty boxcars delivered to the grain elevator, the agent would order them. If Aunt Tilly mailed a fruitcake, the agent would have it waiting in the express room. If the recipient decided to visit the old dear to urge her to give up recreational baking, the same agent would plan the itinerary and sell the tickets.

In November 1951, at the Baltimore & Ohio Railroad depot at Ellicott City, Maryland, a man looks out on the Old Main Line of America's first long-distance railroad. This station on the outskirts of Baltimore was the B&O's first terminus and the destination of the *Tom Thumb*, America's first practical steam engine (1830). The restored station is now a museum.

photo I James P. Gallagher

photo | James P. Gallagher

In this timeless scene, a young boy has ridden his bike to the station to salute a passing Baltimore & Ohio train. Steam has yielded to diesel, but the connection between trains and boys remains as strong as ever.

The agent was among the town's best-known citizens in thousands of small communities. Certainly he was the best-informed person in town. Before radios and long-distance telephones, news spread by telegraph. In most places the station was also the local telegraph office. World events and sports scores, results of national elections and weather forecasts—the agent heard it all first.

The railroads played a leading role in establishing new towns west of the Mississippi River, often spacing them along the main line at 10-mile intervals and frequently naming the new town after a railroad official. The railroad promoted the surrounding land to

potential homesteaders, and the local depot was the railroad's promise that the settlers would still be connected to the wider world. The presence of the railroad meant that tools and supplies could be quickly ordered and cheaply delivered, locally produced crops and manufactured goods could be sold nationwide, and if all else failed (and the majority of homesteaders did fail), the steel rails were an escape route back to civilization.

Stations varied greatly from place to place. The smallest station was sometimes just an unmanned wooden shanty from which the occasional passenger would flag down the train. A mid-sized town handled more travelers and some freight business, so a suitable depot would be warranted. A prosperous resort community or the division point of the railroad would see its importance reflected in a splendid brick or stone building.

When it came to the big cities, railroads pulled out all the stops. The 125-foot-tall vaulted ceiling of Grand Central's main concourse still awes travelers. The union stations built in Kansas City and Washington, D.C., are widely regarded as architectural masterpieces. Chicago's Central and Grand Central stations, had they not fallen to the wrecking ball, would certainly hold similar honors today.

By the 1960s, the American public had nearly abandoned the passenger train. They preferred the flexibility of the automobile for short trips and the speed of the airliner for longer journeys, yet they still had a warm spot in their hearts for railroad stations. The demolition of New York's magnificent Pennsylvania Station in 1962 created such widespread outrage that it is often cited as the beginning of the historic-preservation movement.

Maintaining a respectful distance, a barefoot boy at Cape May, New Jersey, watches a Pennsylvania-Reading Seashore Lines engineer ready his locomotive for a 7:20 a.m. run in August 1952.

photo | James P. Gallagher

Milwaukee Road train number 21, the *Chippewa,* makes a station stop at Coleman, Wisconsin, in 1939. Hardly as grand as the "Grand" terminals, small-town stations were critically important to the future of the nation—and of their communities.

photo | Collection of Clint Jones Jr.

More than a place to arrive and depart, magnificent city train stations like Cincinnati Union Terminal are monuments to civic pride. Was there ever a grander welcome for a weary traveler than a waiting room like this one?

photo | Wallace W. Abbey

photo | Mike Small

Not all railroads joined Amtrak when the government-supported national rail passenger carrier was established in 1971. The Southern Railway was one of the holdouts. In this image, shot at 2:30 a.m. in February 1978, north- and southbound *Southern Crescents* meet at Greensboro, North Carolina. For the trains to meet here, one had to be running more than an hour late— a rare occurrence on the proud Southern.

photo | Paul M. Schmick

In the early 1940s, Washington Union Station had to add 22 ticket windows to cope with the surging demand for travel into and out of the wartime capital. More than 10,000 train tickets were sold daily in the station's Great Hall.

photo | Ed Wojtas

This passenger found a quiet spot to do some reading in the waiting room at Kansas City Union Station.

photo | Wallace W. Abbey

Suitcases in hand, a porter whistles for a cab at New Orleans Union Passenger Terminal on a spring day in 1954.

photo | James G. La Vake

The engineer is walking to the head end as the rest of the crew—conductor, flagman, and coach porter—of Baltimore & Ohio Railroad's *The Cincinnatian* confer beside their train in 1952.

chapter four

Riding the Great Trains

Whether traveling aboard lowly commuter trains or lordly
streamliners, passengers enjoyed rail travel in its heyday

By 1840, the nation had 2,800 miles of railroad track. In his book *American Notes*,
novelist Charles Dickens captured the flavor of an 1842 trip on the Boston &
Lowell Railroad. "On it whirls headlong, dives through the woods again, emerges in
the light, clatters over frail arches, rumbles upon the heavy ground, shoots beneath
a wooden bridge which intercepts the light for a second like a wink, suddenly
awakens all the slumbering echoes in the main street of a large town, and dashes
on haphazard, pell-mell, neck-or-nothing, down the middle of the road."

As the years rolled on, passenger trains became faster, safer, and more
comfortable. In the 50 years between 1865 and 1916, the American rail network
grew from 35,000 miles to more than 250,000 miles. Every town of consequence
had passenger service, and you could take a train from anywhere to anywhere.

In 1902, New York Central launched its luxurious *20th Century Limited* between
New York City and Chicago. Some years later, author Lucius Beebe would write this:
"Showpiece, legend, article of railroad faith, the *20th Century Limited* is a national
institution, moving with the exactitude of sidereal time, as implacable as fate."

When the United States entered World War I in 1917, the nation's railroads were
ill-prepared for a sudden 30 percent increase in business. Debt-laden and over-
regulated, the system was on the verge of chaos when President Woodrow Wilson
ordered the Federal government to take control of 90 of the largest railroads.
By the time railroads returned to private control in 1920, a new form of
transportation had caught the public's fancy. In that year automobile registrations
passed the 8 million mark. In 1928, rail passenger volume was 33 percent lower
than it had been in 1920, and automobile registrations topped 21 million.

The Great Depression compounded the financial difficulties already facing the

Conductor M.R. Adams, who joined the Norfolk
& Western Railway in 1902, uses a lantern to
signal the engineer of the *Pocahontas*.
"Railroading's a lifetime proposition," Adams
said in a 1943 article in *Trains* magazine.
"You've got to live it like I do to enjoy it."

photo Norfolk & Western

railroads. By 1933, rail passenger-miles dipped to a third of the 1920 level, and some railroads were forced into receivership. But there were bright spots in the gloom. In 1935, the Chicago & North Western introduced its *400*, a train named after its schedule, which allowed just 400 minutes to cover the 400 miles between Chicago and Minnesota's Twin Cities. North Western's rivals, the Chicago, Burlington & Quincy and the Milwaukee Road, quickly fielded fast trains of their own.

In the East, New York Central and Pennsylvania Railroad, normally the most bitter of competitors, jointly placed orders for radically new, lightweight, streamlined, air-conditioned passenger cars to re-equip their flagship trains. The Pennsylvania's *Broadway Limited* and the NYC's *20th Century Limited* both entered service on June 15, 1938, with identical 16-hour schedules between New York City and Chicago.

The new trains were undeniably luxurious—the *Century* even had a barbershop. But the railroads no longer had a monopoly on transportation. Highways were improving and millions of cars, trucks, and buses were using them.

Railroads threw themselves wholeheartedly into the war effort in 1941. Freight and passenger business doubled the levels seen during World War I, yet there was no repeat of the confusion of the earlier war, and the government remained on the sidelines.

The end of the war found the railroads ready for a new era. Orders were placed for billions of dollars of new cars and locomotives, including vast numbers of diesel locomotives to replace steam engines. The optimism of the railroad companies extended to passenger service as well. Drab and worn prewar passenger cars were swiftly replaced by gleaming stainless-steel streamliners. A new era in rail travel was at hand, but it would be short-lived.

On October 26, 1958, the Boeing 707 took to the air on its first commercial flight, ushering in the age of jet-powered commercial airline travel. The Highway Act of 1956 authorized $25 billion to build Interstate highways. These developments hit rail travel hard.

By 1960, rail passenger counts were at 20 percent of 1944 levels, and

photo | Pennsylvania Railroad

Dressed to the nines, a woman heads for her seat in a Pennsylvania Railroad coach, a suitcase-laden attendant in her wake.

railroads reported an annual passenger service deficit of $300 million. When the *Century* stopped running in 1967, the railroad's president said that it was the riders, not the company, who had abandoned the train.

With ridership dwindling and no end to the red ink in sight, the Federal government approved the creation of a national passenger rail system in 1970. Amtrak took over the operation of most passenger service in 1971, although a few railroads opted out of the national system and continued to field their own trains for several more years. Amtrak kept a semblance of rail passenger service running and even introduced a few innovations of its own, but the grand era of the streamliner was over.

photo | American Locomotive Co.

With the nation emerging from the rationing and travel restrictions of World War II, railroads prepared for a travel boom, ordering dazzling new passenger equipment. During two days in 1947, these "usherettes" guided more than 15,000 people through a pair of American Locomotive Company diesel locomotives on display at St. Louis Union Station.

photo | Don Wood

With impeccable service and quiet elegance, New York Central's *20th Century Limited* was arguably the greatest train ever. This photograph of the *Century's* signature lounge-observation car was taken in 1962.

photo | Southern Railway

As the 1950s dawned, the Southern Railway joined the rush to equip its fleet of
lightweight, streamlined passenger trains that offered, in the words of a press release
of the time, "travel leisure in a setting of decorative charm."

photo | Chicago, Burlington & Quincy Railroad

The Easter Bunny couldn't make the trip, so Zephyrette Catherine Storrs of the *California Zephyr* distributes baskets of treats Easter morning to the children riding the Chicago–Oakland streamliner.

photo | Pere Marquette

Shortly after World War II, the passenger fleet operated by the Pere Marquette Railway earned the distinction of being the first in the nation to be fully equipped with new streamlined trains offering a winning combination of economical travel and air-conditioned comfort.

The Pullman Company built sleeping cars, and for many decades the company also supplied the crews that took care of those cars. A Pullman conductor, at left, goes over paperwork with a Pennsylvania Railroad conductor who has overall responsibility for the safe and efficient operation of the train.

photo | Pennsylvania Railroad

The round-end observation car was featured on many of the great postwar passenger trains. This couple, possibly escaping a northern winter, has just arrived in the sunny South aboard Southern Railway's newly streamlined *The Southerner*.

With a thunderous roar, excess steam blasts from the locomotive's safety valve as the engineer watches the loading of his train at Southern Pacific's Oakland, California, terminal. Westbound trains to San Francisco arrived not in that great city, but in Oakland, on the eastern shore of San Francisco Bay, where they transferred to ferries bound for their final destination.

photo | Robert Hale

photo | Victor T. Fintak

Dining-Car Service

Burlington Route

This 1898 menu offers an example of the variety of dining choices available to travelers. Prices crept up over the years, but the tradition of good eating on the rails proved enduring.

DINING CAR CRESTON

DINNER

Split Pea Soup, 20c.

Queen Olives, Individual Bottles, 15c.   Assorted Pickles, 10c.

Celery, 15c.

Raw Oysters, half dozen, 25c.

Boiled Salmon, Egg Sauce, 35c.

Boiled Ham and Cabbage, 50c.   Roast Wild Duck, 50c.

Roast Turkey, Cranberry Sauce, 45c.

Prime Roast Beef, 45c.

Rib Ends of Beef, with Brown Potatoes, 35c.

Baked Chicken Pie, 35c.   Baked Pork and Beans, 25c.

Boiled or Mashed Potatoes, 10c.

Braised Sweet Potatoes, 10c.

Sweet Corn, 10c.   Cauliflower, 10c.   Stewed Tomatoes, 10c.

Lobster Salad, 25c.

Pumpkin Pie, 10c.

Apple Pie, 10c.   Plum Pudding, Brandy Sauce, 15c.

Cabinet Pudding, 15c.   Ice Cream, 15c.

Assorted Cake, 15c.

Assorted Fruit in Season, 15c.

Preserved Fruit, Individual Package, 20c.

Roquefort or Club House Cheese, 15c.

Bent's Water Crackers, 10c.

Coffee or Tea, per cup, 10c.

Coffee or Tea, per pot, 25c.

———

NO SERVICE LESS THAN 25 CENTS TO EACH PERSON.

———

Any inattention to duty on this car please report to L. N. Hopkins, Commissary,
C. B. & Q. R. R., Chicago.

———

DENVER ARTESIAN WATER USED ON THESE TABLES.

photo | Chicago, Burlington & Quincy Railroad

Superb meals and elegant place settings helped attract passengers to premier passenger trains, but dining car service was a money-losing proposition for most railroads.

photo | Pennsylvania Railroad

Pennsylvania Railroad's *Congressional* and *Senator* offered fast service between New York and Washington, D.C., and served informal meals in "coffee shop cars"—short-order cooking at its finest. This car was also equipped with a portent of things to come: a microwave oven.

photo | Rock Island Lines

Dining cars like this one provided full-service meals three times a day for the passengers of Rock Island's long distance *Corn Belt* and *Golden State* trains.

From his bouncing and swaying kitchen, barely larger than a walk-in closet, this Milwaukee Road chef, accustomed to the dangers of wielding a knife under such circumstances, prepares superb meals for a trainload of people. A full diner would be staffed by seven or eight men.

photo | Bert Brandt & Associates

A young rider divides her attention between a delicious breakfast and the passing scenery aboard Southern Pacific's *Sunset Limited* in 1961.

photo | Southern Pacific

Before computers, passenger agents booked space on passenger trains by writing down names on the corresponding train manifests and calling agents at other railroads to arrange passage on connecting trains. This photo was taken in October 1950.

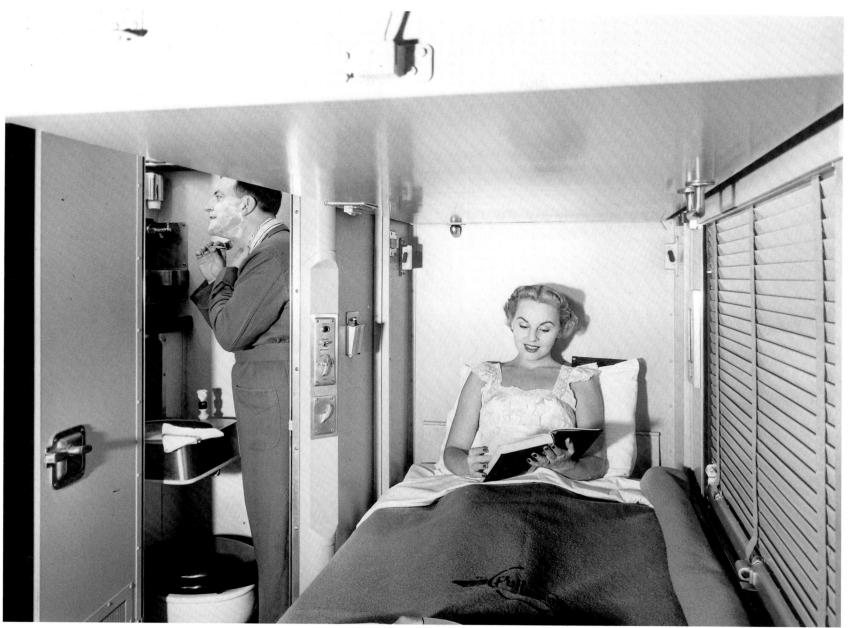

photo | Lawrence S. Williams

Passengers on late-night airline flights may note the comforts of this double-bed compartment and wonder if overnight travel has advanced or declined in the nearly 50 years since this photo was taken. This bedroom had lengthwise berths while some other bedrooms had crosswise berths.

In 1939, the Pennsylvania Railroad inaugurated the overnight *Trail Blazer* with service to Philadelphia, New York, and Chicago. Passengers on the all-coach train were treated to onboard entertainment in the form of radio programs "provided by an instrument of the highest type."

photo | Great Northern Railway

Etched-glass dividers and indirect lighting contribute to the ambiance of the observation car of Great Northern Railway's flagship *Empire Builder*, where passengers enjoy a game of cards.

The Vista-Dome car, a penthouse on wheels, gave passengers a panoramic view of the countryside as well as a forward view, something previously reserved for engineers and firemen.

photo | Seaboard Air Line Railroad

A registered nurse aboard the Seaboard Air Line Railroad's flagship *Silver Meteor* checks her supplies as the train prepares to depart Miami for a run to New York City. Before commercial air travel became popular, several railroads used the term "air line" to express the concept of the shortest line between two points.

photo | Pennsylvania Railroad

Vast train sheds protected passengers from rain and snow. The shed at Pennsylvania Railroad's Broad Street Station in Philadelphia sheltered commuter and short-distance intercity passengers below a 100-foot arched vault that reflected the importance the railroad attached to its headquarters city. The photograph shows platform repairs after a 1923 fire. The shed itself, heavily damaged, was removed not long after this photograph was made.

chapter five

The Guiding Hand

Dispatchers, tower operators, and railroad officials directed an empire from behind the scenes

Often the most difficult jobs in railroading are performed in places far removed from the noise and smoke of a locomotive cab. Keeping trains flowing smoothly, safely, and quickly falls on the shoulders of dispatchers and tower operators, trainmasters and division superintendents, presidents and vice presidents.

Dispatchers, classified as members of management on some railroads and non-management on others, form the base of the control structure. Like a chess player, a dispatcher plans his strategy many moves in advance but with a gambler's eye for playing the odds and seizing unexpected openings. The dispatcher's job is one of intense pressure and concentration. Speed is of the essence, but mistakes can have deadly consequences.

Today, a dispatcher at a computerized console throws far-distant switches and changes trackside signals with a mouse, and he uses a radio to talk with crews. But for many years dispatchers used long pieces of paper called "train sheets" to keep track of trains moving across their territory, and the telegraph to send instructions to stations and towers for relay to passing trains. The system seems primitive today, but it was well considered, had effective safeguards, and was continually fine-tuned. It worked well for decades.

The operator standing his lonely watch in far-flung stations and towers was the essential link between the dispatcher at his telegraph key and the train crew. When the telegraph sounder hammered out his station's code, he had to be ready to type. Rolling the typed orders into a tight cylinder, he knotted them with a loop of string and attached the string to a wooden hoop. He made one hoop for the engine crew, and a second hoop for the caboose, both with identical orders. As the train approached, the operator stood inches from the rail,

The development of Centralized Traffic Control allowed dispatchers like Santa Fe's Harry Flottman to control train movements over a far-flung territory. From his desk in Newton, Kansas, as this vintage photo shows, he is in the process of clearing a signal on the high-speed freight line that carries transcontinental traffic around the outskirts of Newton and Wichita. A track diagram runs the length of the top of the machine. Its lights indicate train locations, the direction the switches are set, and the color of the trackside signal. Trains can operate in both directions on the same track using sidings to pass.

photo | Wallace W. Abbey

holding the hoop high in the air. Crouching low in the open door of the rushing engine, a brakeman or fireman stretched out a crooked arm and snagged the string and its orders. A hundred or so cars later, the operator repeated the performance as the caboose swept past.

Dispatchers and operators are two examples of a multitude of railroad jobs—from the president of the railroad down to front-line managers—involving the control and management of a large and dynamic industry. A 1914 textbook describes the division of duties on one major railroad: "In brief, on the Norfolk & Western it may be said that the first vice president gets the business, the second vice president moves it, and the third vice president collects and pays the bills and keeps the records." The vice presidents report to the railway president, who in turn answers to the board of directors.

The management style follows a nearly military chain of command. The builder of the eastern half of the nation's first transcontinental railroad, General Grenville Dodge, noted the following in his memoirs. "The organization for the construction of the Union Pacific Railway was purely upon a military basis. Nearly every man working upon it had been in the Civil War; the heads of most of the engineering parties and all of the construction forces were officers in the Civil War; the chief of the track-laying force, General Casement, had been a division commander in the Civil War; and at any moment I could call into the field a thousand men, well-officered, ready to meet any crisis or emergency."

Trends in management styles have come and gone in most industries, but railroads remain organized in ways that General Dodge would recognize and approve. Each level answers directly to the level above, yet each manager has precisely defined responsibilities and wields absolute authority within that area. Railroads are huge operations governed from central offices that can be thousands of miles distant, but the freedom of line managers to take immediate independent action allows the organization to react with startling speed and flexibility in a crisis.

photo | Richard Steinheimer

In this August 1952 photo, a Southern Pacific operator at Saugus, California, bangs out train orders for an eastbound freight. Orders were typed on a very thin paper that railroaders called "flimsies."

photo | O. Winston Link Trust

Hager Tower in Hagerstown, Maryland, guarded the crossing of the Norfolk & Western, Western Maryland, and Pennsylvania tracks and provided a comfortable place for waiting crews to warm themselves on a winter's night and catch up on the latest gossip.

photo | Chicago, Burlington & Quincy

Copies of orders issued to train crews hang from nails in the Chicago, Burlington & Quincy
Railroad's division office in Galesburg, Illinois, in May 1948.

The engine crew of a Baltimore & Ohio Railroad eastbound train receives written orders "on the fly" as they depart the yard at Connellsville, Pennsylvania, in August 1954.

Southern Pacific Trainmaster Rufus E. Dipprey started work everyday at 7 a.m. Quitting time depended on events—during a 1957 flood he worked 52 hours without sleep. He was responsible for keeping trains running smoothly across his far-flung territory. Here Dipprey inspects a conductor's watch to make sure it is keeping the correct time.

photo | Clyde Carley

Trainmaster Rufus Dipprey presides over an oral rules exam for three switchmen. The exam tests their knowledge of the numerous special instructions printed in the division's timetable. Oral exams lasted as long as 12 hours with only a break for lunch. A passing score was 80 percent or higher.

photo | Clyde Carley

photo | Henry J. McCord

This Chicago, Burlington & Quincy crew caller has the daunting task of scheduling crews for outbound trains. Under terms of labor agreements, employees with the most seniority get first crack at plum assignments.

Anticipating the arrival of an evening train in 1961, the Rutland Railroad station agent at Bennington, Vermont, walks outside to hang red lanterns on the railroad's ancient ball-type signal. Ball signals were among the earliest systems for controlling train movements. When the engineer saw the light from the lanterns all the way at the top of the post, he would open the throttle wide knowing the track ahead was clear. Although ball signals were eventually replaced by color light signals, the term "highball" remains a part of the everyday language of railroaders and means "get moving."

photo | Jim Shaughnessy

Working in concert, operators at Lake Street Tower control the switches and signals leading into Chicago & North Western Railway's Chicago terminal. The four men assigned to this tower typically handled 82 train movements during rush hour using this interlocking machine, so-called because its levers "interlocked" to prevent conflicting routes from being selected. Sixty-six of the levers on this machine control trackside signals; the remaining 104 levers operate switches that route trains from one track to another.

photo | Chicago & North Western Railway

Operators manning remote train-order stations, like this one on the Southern Pacific's Willamette Pass line at Cascade Summit, Oregon, lived in near-complete isolation for long tours of duty, but their surroundings could be breathtakingly beautiful.

photo | Southern Pacific Railroad

photo | Richard J. Cook

Railroad managers for the Pittsburg & Shawmut inspect the railroad from the comfort of their "business car," an automobile equipped with steel railroad wheels. One suspects that the junior member of the management team gets the job of turning the car at Freeport, Pennsylvania.

photo | Wayne E. Davenport

Hoops for handing up orders to passing trains hang on the wall, and the typewriter is at the ready should the dispatcher telegraph an order. This young operator is working the late-night "third trick" shift at the station in Port Kent, New York, in August 1949.

The Rights of Trains

By Mark W. Hemphill
Editor, *Trains* Magazine

This photograph of Western Pacific dispatcher Peter Josserand exemplifies the art and creed of dispatching. He has in front of him nothing but a train sheet, a pen, a telephone, and a telegraph key, yet he is making the decisions that make his railroad run. He holds in his head the power to run his railroad efficiently or poorly, safely or dangerously, proudly or with bitterness and strife.

The job of train dispatcher has remained essentially unchanged for more than 100 years. Train dispatchers are the men and women who execute the company's basic operating strategy by determining when trains will run, the specific meeting and passing points, and the precedence of trains, switching, or track maintenance work. To a large extent, the quality of dispatching makes or breaks a railroad.

Dispatching is fundamentally an intellectual profession that requires the ability to project complex patterns hours or even days into the future. Unlike a highway or the sky, a railroad track can accommodate only one train at a time. To occupy a main track (as opposed to a yard track or industrial spur), a train must be granted authority. The dispatcher is the person who grants that authority—or takes it away. The authority springs from "the rules," a large book of detailed instructions tested in the fire of experience and disaster, and rewritten constantly.

Variance from the rules is the root cause of most wrecks, derailments, injuries, and fatalities in railroading. The careless or incompetent dispatcher who violates the rules will be disciplined immediately, and if violations continue, he will be fired. Dispatchers can make—and have made—disastrous mistakes or oversights that have killed people. The mistake can be as small as not paying close attention to a conductor's repeat of a verbal instruction.

The dispatcher consults with the chief dispatcher, trainmasters, and yardmasters to determine when and what trains will be run, issues

photo | Peter Josserand

Peter Josserand, night chief dispatcher of the Western Pacific Railroad, updated *The Rights of Trains*, first published in 1904, a book that established the principles of safe and efficient train operations.

instructions to the crew callers to call a crew for each train, issues the work plan to the train crew when they arrive to register for their train, and directs the train crews to proceed, stop, take a siding, or do other work en route.

The dispatcher works with dispatchers on other railroads whose tracks intersect or abut to coordinate hand-offs. He grants time on the main track to maintainers and track inspectors, informs the signal department of signal failures and grade-crossing gates that have malfunctioned (usually, a car has crashed through them), and handles myriad other unforeseen events, calamities, and occurrences.

The dispatcher is locked into a brutal conflict with the clock. He must work quickly (but meticulously), and time is always running out on him. It's not uncommon for a dispatcher to never get up from his desk, even for a bathroom break. On a busy desk, a dispatcher will answer 250 or more radio and telephone calls daily; often 10 or more requests are lit up at once.

In most cases, dispatchers do their job without ever seeing face-to-face the train crews, maintainers, yardmasters, and trainmasters they work with. In a full career a dispatcher may never meet some of the people he talks to every day.

Their communication is entirely by telephone, radio, and fax machine; their view of the world isn't the reality the train crew sees from the locomotive cab, but a representation. The dispatcher's territory might be represented by a schematic diagram on a computer screen, with line segments lit up to indicate which tracks are occupied. Or dispatchers might just work on a ruled piece of paper—the train sheet—with the numbers and information about the trains on their territories and the track segment each is authorized to occupy. In other words, the job of a train dispatcher consists almost entirely of a mental picture. He builds, updates, and manipulates to consider thousands of future possibilities.

Yet dispatchers are not dispassionate voices on the radio or telephone. Train crews quickly learn their voices, idiosyncrasies, and abilities—the last-mentioned especially important because train crews are usually paid by the mile, not by the hour. Crews discover if a particular dispatcher is fair or thoughtless, in control or easily pushed around, skilled at getting trains over the road as quickly as possible, or hopelessly inept—and they share that information with each other.

Each dispatcher works a specific territory, traditionally known as "a desk" and often today as "a console." Each desk requires five dispatchers, each with staggered days off. Three dispatchers cover the days, afternoons, and midnights, five days a week. A relief dispatcher covers their "weekends," working two days followed by two afternoons and one midnight, and an "extra-board," or fill-in dispatcher, picks up the one remaining midnight plus vacation and sick days of the regular

dispatchers. Dating to 1905, dispatchers are restricted by Federal law to working no more than 9 hours in every 24.

Traditionally, dispatchers came out of the ranks of train-order operators, the men and women who typed up dispatchers' instructions to trains and handed them up to engineers and conductors. Today, operators have virtually vanished, and dispatchers are promoted from other jobs, such as clerks or conductors and engineers that want an inside job with predictable hours. All go through an extensive training program to learn the rules and the dispatching software a particular railroad uses, followed by an apprenticeship lasting as long as nine months. The apprenticeship consists of the trainee sitting with an experienced dispatcher to learn the job through observation and question, monitoring the radio and telephone conversation through a headset without a microphone. In time, the trainee is allowed to run the desk, with the dispatcher watching like a hawk. Any mistake made by the trainee is the responsibility of the dispatcher; both will be fired for a large one.

As the dispatcher gains confidence in the trainee, the apprentice is left on his own for longer periods, and if he does well—that is, if he makes no major rule violations and doesn't delay too many trains too badly—he's judged ready to "mark-up," i.e., work on his own. A sizeable proportion of new dispatchers never mark-up, or, if they do, are fired for cause or quit within a year. Heart attacks, high blood pressure, and other stress-disorders are common; it's not uncommon for dispatchers to suffer nervous breakdowns, divorce, and shortened lifespans.

Yet despite the stresses and frustrations, those who love railroads gravitate toward dispatching more than any other job on the railroad. No greater satisfaction exists than that of seeing a complex and risky plan come together to near-perfection, and often a dispatcher hangs around the desk after his hand-off to the next dispatcher to see how his plan unfolds—and only those who have worked as a dispatcher will ever completely appreciate the beauty of their designs.

chapter six

The Permanent Way

Back-breaking work by an army of men built and maintained the railroad

To understand the job of the track worker, it helps to understand the most vital component of any railroad—the track. Track is an elegant system of layers that supports and guides immensely heavy moving trains. The weight of the train presses on steel rails which transmit the weight to cross ties. The ties spread the weight broadly and redistribute it to a layer of coarse stone ballast, which is supported by a still-wider base of sub-ballast resting on a roadbed made level by filling low points and cutting down high areas. The ties also hold the rails in proper position, and the ballast drains away water, while its inherent flexibility absorbs frost heaves and other stresses that might throw the track out of alignment.

Thanks to long experience with all these materials, railroads have precise standards for every part of track. For example, igneous rock, such as granite, quartz, or feldspar, or a hard sedimentary rock such as limestone, is considered the best for ballast. To pass muster, ballast must be clean, uniform in size and quality, and have an angular shape to pack closely under the ties yet drain freely.

Specific requirements also exist for ties, but the railroads reserve their toughest standards for rails. Consider the drop test. A six-foot section of rail is cut from the first rail rolled from each ingot of steel. The sample rail is placed on two supports, four feet apart. A one-ton weight is then dropped on the unsupported middle of the sample from a height of 22 feet. If the rail does not break, all the rails rolled from that ingot are considered to have met the standard.

Good materials are critical, but it is the maintenance-of-way crews that keep the railroad running safely and efficiently. Replacing rotted ties and worn rails, removing snow and cutting back vegetation—the work never ends. Over the years the tasks have become more mechanized, but not easier.

James S. Begay, a Navajo track worker on a Santa Fe Railway road gang, uses a pair of tie tongs to move a new tie into position near Winslow, Arizona.

photo | Santa Fe Railway

photo | Jim Shaughnessy

On a blizzard-swept night in 1958, a section man on the Troy Union Railway melts the snow around switch points by pouring burning oil on the track in preparation for the arrival of Boston & Maine train number 59, *The Minuteman*, from Boston.

photo | John S. Ingles, collection of J. David Ingles

Creative scrounging and a willingness to make do with limited resources kept many a short line afloat. The section gang of the Midland Railway poses with visiting railroad enthusiasts outside the engine house at Newark, Illinois, in September 1946 with their homemade track car and trailer.

Track workers take turns swinging spike mauls. An experienced man's fluid circular swings looked effortless. Steel met steel in ringing blows as steady as the ticking of a clock.

photo | Norfolk & Western Railway

A machine has ground a flat and level surface across these ties in preparation for new rail. The gang brushes on creosote wood preservative. They'll place tie plates next, then spike down the new rail.

photo | Donald Sims

With a varied assortment of hand tools at his feet, the foreman of a Southern Pacific track gang ponders the blueprint for the installation of a new switch.

photo | Chicago & North Western Railway

Assembling the complex geometry of heavy-duty moving parts that make up a switch demanded a mixture of exacting precision and raw physical strength unique to railroading.

As shown in this 1955 photo, a lining-bar gang uses long steel bars to adjust track in an amazing display of coordinated force. The caller, standing at right, is famed for his rich, clear voice and his vast repertoire of often-comic two-line songs. When the foreman signals the direction to shift the track, the caller sings, and the combined strength of the gang pulling in time to the music moves the track.

photo | Norfolk & Western Railway

photo | New Haven Railroad

The lighthouse tender *Tulip* came to rest on the New York, New Haven & Hartford Railroad's main line at New London, Connecticut, during the hurricane of September 21, 1936. Moving the *Tulip* was just one in a long list of obstacles to reopening the storm-ravaged railroad. Other damages included 31 bridges and 200 culverts destroyed, and track washed away in numerous places across the system. In just 13 days, rail service was restored between Boston and New York City.

photo | New Haven Railroad

Five thousand cars of gravel and stone were needed to repair damage
caused by the 1936 hurricane. On this line alone, 75 miles of track had
been destroyed or damaged by high water. Here workers have moved the
track back into alignment and are dumping ballast to support the track.

The San Diego & Arizona Railway was dismissed by critics as "the impossible railroad," and they had the facts on their side. Building a direct line from San Diego to the east required a right-of-way chipped out of solid granite across one of the most forbidding landscapes imaginable. The 11-mile stretch through Carriso Gorge alone required 17 tunnels as well as numerous bridges and side-hill trestles. In this photo, keeping the railroad open is the job of Bill Waters, who patrols the line in his track speeder. This line is now long-closed, though much of the track still exists, and efforts are underway to reopen parts of the route as a tourist destination.

photo | Richard Steinheimer

photo | New York Central Railroad

The "Tenth Avenue Cowboy" was a familiar sight in 1941 on the streets of New York City's west side, where a local ordinance required a rider to warn automobile traffic in advance of New York Central trains delivering to warehouses and running on tracks laid in the street.

photo | Al Rung

A painter brushes silver on an already immaculate Santa Fe bridge in Los Angeles.

chapter seven

Yard Work

When it came to moving freight, yards and the men who worked them made it happen

Seeing a train rolling along the main line is like walking in and out of a theater halfway through a movie. You've missed the beginning and the ending. Yards are the beginnings and endings of railroads; they are not glorified parking lots where cars and locomotives sit for days on end.

Yards are sorting machines. Trains arrive, the road locomotives are removed and taken away for servicing, and the train's cars are sorted according to destination. For example, one track in the yard might be reserved for cars bound for Chicago. As trains arrive and are broken down (disassembled), all the Chicago-bound cars eventually wind up on that track.

At regular intervals the cars are assembled into trains. If the railroad's line to Chicago passes through Milwaukee, all the cars from the Milwaukee track might be added to the train, along with cars for other cities en route. The cars are coupled together, air brake hoses attached, the train is inspected for defects, road locomotives arrive from the roundhouse and are coupled on, a rested crew climbs aboard, and the train is on its way.

Other considerations come into play. A train of refrigerated meat needs to get to its destination swiftly and will not be assigned to pick up and drop off cars along the way. Instead, a lower-priority train is assigned the task of picking up and dropping off cars in cities and towns on that route.

In the railroad industry, freight pays the bills. The faster that cars are sorted and back on the road, the sooner the freight will be delivered and the empty car freed for another customer. For that reason, railroads spend a great deal of time and money boosting the speed and efficiency of yard operations.

Two types of yards exist: flat and gravity. In a flat yard, a switch engine

On a summer night in 1955 at the Baltimore & Ohio Railroad's Riverside Yard in Baltimore, Maryland, a railroader ponders a board listing the locomotives that need to be serviced for tomorrow's trains.

photo | James P. Gallagher

connects to the rear of a string of cars to be sorted. It pushes the cars at the forward end to their classification track, uncouples them, and backs the remaining cars out. Switches are thrown and the engine pushes the next cars to their classification track. Eventually the inbound cars are properly sorted, but the back-and-forth movements are time-consuming.

Gravity-switched yards, also called "hump yards," are more expensive to build than flat yards, but they are much more efficient. In a gravity yard, inbound cars are shoved by a switch engine up a manmade hill. The cars are uncoupled at the top of the hill and roll freely down into the main body of the yard. Remote-controlled switches route the car to its classification track.

If its destination track is nearly full, a freely rolling car will strike the other cars at too great a rate of speed. In the early days, brakemen rode the cars down hill, controlling speed by tightening the hand-turned brakewheel. In time, an automated braking system called a "retarder" was developed. With this system, as the cars crested the hump, they would be automatically weighed. As they started to roll downgrade, a device measured their rate of acceleration as they approached the retarder system. A light car bound for an empty track would need little or no braking, while a heavy car bound for a crowded track required considerable braking.

In addition to the classification tracks, yards have tracks for repairing cars damaged in transit and for storing cabooses between runs. Other tracks are intended for engine servicing—in the days of steam, they led to the roundhouse, sand tower, ash pit, and the coal and water supplies.

Passenger trains have their own designated yard and engine facilities, generally located as close as possible to the terminal so they can be swiftly cleaned, serviced, and resupplied between runs.

photo | Southern Railway

Stogie clenched in his teeth, Thomas Frederick "Jack" Pearson, a veteran brakeman at Southern Railway's yard in Spencer, North Carolina, pauses while throwing a switch to have his portrait taken by the company photographer.

photo | W.A. Akin, Jr.

A car inspector on the Chesapeake & Ohio Railway at Danville, West Virginia, uses a hook to arrange oil-soaked packing material around the axle of a coal hopper car in this 1956 photo. The oil is drawn up into the bearing area by wheel motion, and the weight of the car—30 tons over a few square inches—is carried on a film of lube oil. If the journal runs dry, the bearing will overheat and possibly cause a derailment. The chore of checking the packing and lubricating journal boxes was a never-ending task in the days before roller-bearing-equipped cars became common.

photo | Southern Pacific

The tower is a railroad yard's nerve center. Here, Southern Pacific assistant yardmaster R.K. McAlister is building outbound trains by telling crews on the ground which cars to pull from the classification tracks.

Railroads run on coal, oil, and most of all, paperwork. Clerks in the Southern Pacific yard office in Fresno, California, are busy filling out tags, switch lists, and other reports necessary for handling trains through that terminal.

Before widespread use of parcel shipping companies like UPS, the railroads were often assigned the task of transporting packages across the country. Here, the platform foreman at the car door checks the details of a shipment as carts loaded with cargo slowly move past (foreground). The carts have hinged arms that connect to an under-floor "Towveyor" that slowly pulls the carts in a loop through the freight house. A checker assigns a destination number to each boxcar and chalks the same number on carts bound for that destination. As the carts move through the freight house, they are pulled off at their car by stow men.

photo | New York Central

Railroads handled shipments ranging from a single carton to an entire boxcar load. At New York Central's freight house in Utica, N.Y., a platoon of drivers on self-propelled trucks, forklifts, a portable crane, tractors, and other equipment kept the cargo moving.

photo | Union Pacific Railroad

Although the railroads didn't relish the competition for freight, they quickly realized the efficiencies of loading a truck trailer at the shipper and delivering the trailer directly to the customer's loading dock. They went truckers one better by placing the trailers on flatcars and moving them across country dozens at a time.

Neatness counts, especially when the residue of a previous cargo might damage a future load. This 1950 photograph shows the tank car cleaning facility at Hobart Yard in Los Angeles.

photo | Santa Fe Railway

photo | Southern Pacific Railroad

D.W. Morris, Southern Pacific's supervisor of signal construction, tests a gravity-switched-yard's automatic relay panel. The circuits control the switching of cars after the track has been lined for a specific movement. Another set of relays governs the automatic track brakes that slow the cars as they move down the hill and into the classification tracks of the yard.

photo | Donald Sims

When trains enter a yard, the cars can be flat-switched (pushed and pulled to their respective tracks) or gravity-switched, as is the case in this Southern Pacific facility. Gravity switching involves releasing one or more cars at a time to roll down a hill while an operator in the tower—shown here at right—switches the moving cars to their proper tracks. The car retarders, track-mounted brake devices, can be seen just ahead of the lead boxcar.

To prevent engineers from moving a train unexpectedly—while a repair is still underway, for example—maintenance workers place blue flags in the front window of a locomotive before they start a task. The engineer isn't allowed to move a train when a blue flag is in place, and only the employee that put it there can remove it. Here, car inspector George Myers has just removed his blue flag from the cab of locomotive 926 during a snow storm in Harrisburg, Pennsylvania, on February 6, 1978, indicating that he has completed his work and the locomotive is ready to go.

photo | Jim Bradley

photo | Pennsylvania Railroad

To keep their passengers fed, railroads maintained commissary buildings at their passenger coach yards in major cities. This commissary in Chicago featured several room-sized refrigerators. Food handling has changed since this photo was taken, but passenger trains still need to be stocked.

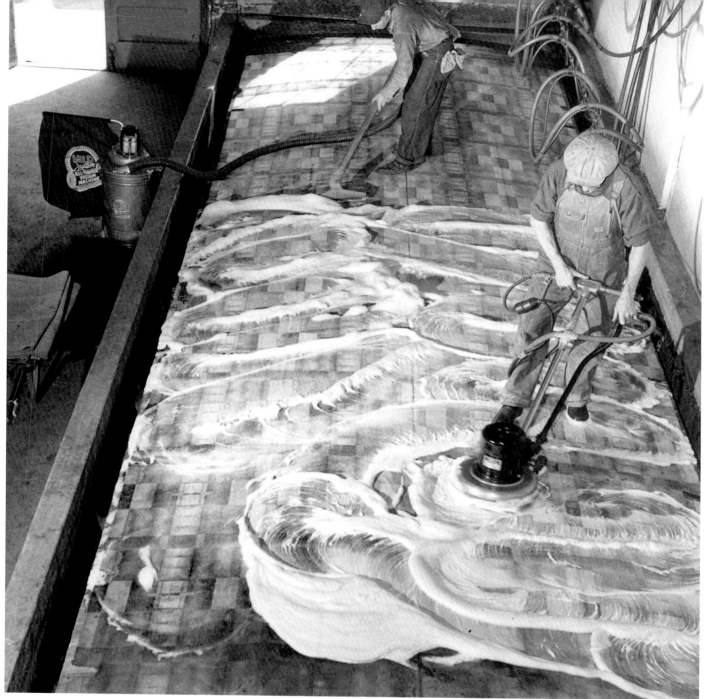

photo | Santa Fe Railway

Passenger car carpeting requires cleaning as often as once a week. The carpets are removed from the car, and the rug cleaners get to work. One man, using a revolving brush fed with cleaning solution, applies a heavy layer of cleanser. After his partner vacuums up the solution, the rug is placed in a special drying compartment.

On a foggy morning in 1948 at Grand Central Station in Houston, Texas, a switchman, nattily attired in felt hat and tie, signals the crew of a Southern Pacific locomotive. The engine has just arrived with train No. 5, the *Argonaut*, from New Orleans and is being switched to go to the roundhouse for servicing.

photo | LeRoy Wilkie

chapter eight

Roundhouse and Back Shop

Some of America's most skilled craftsmen tended to the care and feeding of steam and diesel iron horses

In 1830, the *Tom Thumb*, a tiny four-wheeled steam locomotive, ran a race against a horse. The outcome would decide if the Baltimore & Ohio Railroad, which was then using real horsepower to pull its coaches, would switch to steam locomotion. The little engine broke down and the horse won at a trot, but B&O officials could nonetheless see the potential of steam.

Just over a century later, in 1941, the American Locomotive Works released the first of 25 new steam locomotives built for the Union Pacific and nicknamed them "Big Boys." The *Tom Thumb* weighed 1 ton and couldn't beat a single horse; the Big Boys weighed 540 tons and produced 6,290 horsepower.

Locomotives had come a long way since the first steam engine experiments. The Big Boy was 133 feet long, 16 feet high, and 11 feet wide; the tender held 32 tons of coal and 24,000 gallons of water. The locomotive's firebox alone was the size of a one-car garage. The Big Boys were aptly named.

Just as impressive was the roundhouse and backshop complex at Cheyenne, Wyoming, where Union Pacific typically maintained and serviced some 50 steam locomotives. After each run, the locomotives cut off from their trains and clanked slowly along the service tracks to the massive steel coal dock—one of the largest ever built—spanning five tracks. Here ash and cinders were emptied from the fireboxes into pits between the rails, the tenders were filled with tons of coal, and sand (sprayed on the rails to improve traction) was added to the sand domes. The tender water tanks were topped off at one of the servicing area's several water columns, and then the engines were washed. At that point the locomotives were finally placed in roundhouse stalls to await their next runs.

Steam locomotives due for an overhaul, or locomotives that required extensive

Norfolk & Western locomotive 2165 stands astride the inspection pit in the railroad's Iaeger, West Virginia, shops in March 1959. The N&W held on to its steam engines longer than most railroads, but the inevitable diesels would be arriving soon and end the era when an army of skilled craftsmen kept the wheels of commerce turning.

photo Bruce R. Meyer

or complex repair work, were sent to the backshop—a collective term for the vast array of large and small buildings behind the Cheyenne roundhouse. Here locomotive boilers were lifted from their wheels by a 250-ton overhead crane and taken to the boiler shop to be disassembled, cleaned, and rebuilt. At the same time, an army of skilled mechanics took apart the running gear. New parts were built and worn ones mended on row after row of machine tools.

Employing 5,000 people, the sprawling Cheyenne Shops were typical of the steam shops operated by major railroads. Roundhouse and backshop workers were some of the most highly skilled craftsmen in America. They had to be—steam locomotives were high-maintenance machines with few interchangeable parts.

Big Boys were enormous pieces of moving machinery. They were, in the precise sense of the word, awesome. Few sights in railroading could match the drama of a Big Boy storming up Sherman Hill west of Cheyenne with a heavy train. The show lasted 20 years and then the Big Boys were gone, along with thousands of other steam locomotives across the nation, swept aside by diesel-electric locomotives.

Diesels do more work with less fuel. Diesels also require less maintenance and are more flexible in operation. The diesel's efficiency came with a human price tag. It was the roundhouse and backshop workers who felt the biggest impact of the diesel.

Cheyenne provides an example. The immense complex of shops has nearly vanished. Today a handful of railroaders perform various support tasks where 5,000 once toiled.

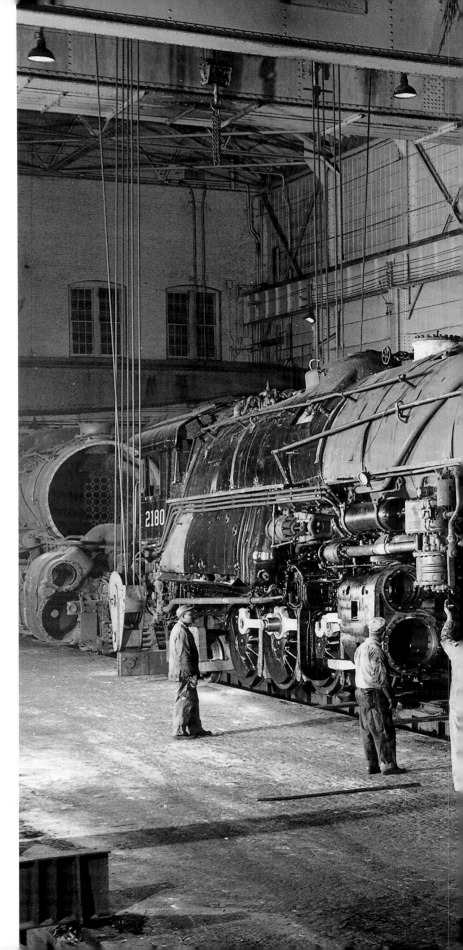

In a process called "wheeling," a massive overhead crane gingerly sets the boiler of a Norfolk & Western class Y6 on its 12 driving wheels during the locomotive's annual overhaul. Wheeling was usually performed late at night so that the locomotive would be ready to be worked on in the morning when a hundred or more expert mechanics would arrive. Within 24 hours this locomotive would be back in service.

photo | O. Winston Link Trust

photo | Robert Hale

A welder fuses the ends of boiler tubes inside the cavernous firebox of a Norfolk & Western steam locomotive. When this space is filled with tons of white-hot burning coal, the draft created by the locomotive stack will draw the intensely hot combustion gases from the firebox into these tubes that run the length of the boiler. The water surrounding the tubes in the boiler is heated, creating steam to power the locomotive.

photo | H. Franklin Lange

Roundhouses were often built with large expanses of glass windows to take advantage of natural lighting. In Milwaukee, Wisconsin, the sun's rays slanting through the perpetual haze of smoke produced this dramatic portrait of Milwaukee Road steam at rest in 1953.

photo | Richard Steinheimer

With the locomotive stripped of its steel jacketing and blanket of insulation, a team of mechanics in Southern Pacific's General Shops in Sacramento, California, replace the flexible bolts that support the firebox. Steam locomotives captured the imagination like no other machine before or since, but when diesel builders promised reduced maintenance, railroads listened.

photo | Charles W. Martz

A big job requires big tools. At the Pennsylvania Railroad's Williamsport, Pennsylvania, roundhouse
in 1951, machinist Ed S. Nau is making a temporary repair to the running gear of a locomotive.
It will soon be taken to the main shops for a complete overhaul.

photo | Philip R. Hastings

Two laborers disassemble the running gear of a Pennsylvania Railroad locomotive at Renovo, Pennsylvania. Mechanics often used the cylinder jacket as a sort of notebook for ongoing work.

A machinist confers with a co-worker who is inside the locomotive's frame in order to remove a broken equalizer rod. Replacing the rod will be dirty and exhausting, and these men are working with a heightened sense of urgency because this engine is scheduled to pull a fast freight in a few hours.

photo | Paul H. Gillem

After ruling the rails for more than a century, steam was replaced by diesel locomotives in a breathtakingly short time. Diesels, like this one being lowered onto its trucks at General Motors' Electro-Motive Division plant in LaGrange, Illinois, required fewer workers to maintain and operate them. Sentimentality wasn't part of the balance sheet.

photo | Kalmbach collection

photo | Milwaukee Road

A rebuilt 1,500-horsepower diesel engine is lowered into the car body of a Milwaukee Road locomotive at Milwaukee, Wisconsin. The same locomotive earlier received a reconditioned main generator, which can be glimpsed behind the man standing on the walkway. In a diesel-electric locomotive, the engine turns the generator, which supplies electricity to motors mounted on the axles.

photo | American Locomotive Co.

This February 1956 photo shows a shop technician using a king-sized caliper to check the bearing on the massive crankshaft of an 1,800-horsepower diesel engine.

photo | W.A. Akin Jr.

Locomotives keep the railroad moving, but freight cars pay the bills. These Chesapeake & Ohio
Railway men have the hard and debilitating task of riveting together the body of a coal hopper car.

photo | American Car & Foundry

The critical part of any freight car is the bearing surface of the axle. Machinists like this one at American Car & Foundry's Huntington, West Virginia, plant produced axles with tolerances that would do credit to a watchmaker.

photo | American Car & Foundry

A banner on the covered hopper car notes the milestone—the 3,000th impact test conducted
at American Car & Foundry's St. Charles, Missouri Technical Center. Rolling the car down the
ramp into the fully loaded freight car standing on the shop floor generates 1.5 million pounds
of coupling impact force. Should anything break during this test, which mimics the stresses of
everyday railroad service, American Car & Foundry engineers will know what needs to be redesigned.

photo | George De Koven

Steam engines were finicky about the quality of water they boiled. Scale buildup in the boiler tubes could cripple an engine; other components in water could cause foaming inside the boiler.
Here K.P. Howe, assistant engineer of water supply, watches service engineer P.J. Dempsey test the alkalinity of the water at Union Station in Louisville, Kentucky, in 1941.

One of several innovations that allowed rapid mass-production of diesel locomotives is found in this two-story-high Ingersoll angle-boring machine that bores rough and finished holes in a diesel locomotive cylinder block. This cylinder block will go into the long hood of a diesel locomotive.

photo | American Locomotive Co.

On the shop floor at the American Locomotive Works in Schenectady, New York, workers use a winch to lift one of the pistons into the 12-cylinder engine block. With each piston weighing several hundred pounds, that winch is critical to getting the job done without damaging the part.

Henry Ford's use of the assembly line to produce Model T cars in the early years of the twentieth century expanded to all sorts of manufacturing. By the 1950s, General Motors' Electro-Motive Division was using an assembly line system to produce complete locomotive cab assemblies at its Plant No. 2 in Chicago, Illinois.

photo | Seaboard Air Line Railroad

Diesel locomotives required new skills to keep them in running order. Here a Seaboard Air Line Railroad electrician winds copper wire around the armature of a locomotive's traction motor.

When this photograph was taken in 1949, diesels handled 19 percent of the New York Central's passenger trains and 13 percent of its freight trains, and the railroad had orders on the books for $33.6 million of new diesels.

photo | New York Central

With an up-and-down wave of his lantern, a trainman signals the engineer to start a trio of General Electric U25B diesels rolling.

photo | General Electric

A mechanic checks the locomotive work schedule board in Union Pacific's Cheyenne, Wyoming, roundhouse in 1957.

photo | Philip R. Hastings

In October 1955, Boston & Maine train director R.P. Fonda lights a kerosene lantern used to signal trains to stop and pick up written orders at JV Tower in Johnsonville, New York.

photo | Jim Shaughnessy

A railroader heading into the sunset uses a lit "fusee," similar to a highway emergency flare, to signal a Southern Pacific locomotive at Ben Ali yard near Sacramento, California, in November 1952.

photo | Jim Morley

Afterword from the Author

Pioneering photojournalist Robert Doisneau said, "A hundredth of a second here, a hundredth of a second there—even if you put them end to end, they still only add up to one, two, perhaps three seconds, snatched from eternity." In closing this work, I am again struck by the power of these photographs. The images represent just a few seconds in the history of America's greatest industry, and show us just a handful of faces from the tens of thousands who spent their working lives on the railroad. Yet these infinitesimal moments of time have much to teach us.

Many of the photographers whose work is found in these pages are no longer with us. In some instances, even their names could not be learned. But their work endures and it is an honor to present their images in these pages. Several people graciously agreed to share their photographs and I would particularly like to thank Betty Kimball, Jim Shaughnessy, Wayne Leeman, J. Parker Lamb Jr., Don Wood, Jeff Brouws, Shirley Burman and Richard Steinheimer, Mike Small, Salem Tamer of the O. Winston Link Trust, J. David Ingles, Donald Sims, Jim Bradley, and Bruce R. Meyer.

A photographer sees, the camera records, and fleeting reality becomes a work of art for later generations to appreciate. Through these images we gain a fresh understanding of the enduring dignity of labor. To these photographers we owe a great debt.

January 2004
Milwaukee, Wis.